NEAR & FAR

INTERIORS I LOVE

NEAR & FAR

INTERIORS I LOVE

LISA FINE

PHOTOGRAPHY BY
MIGUEL FLORES-VIANNA

FOREWORD BY
DEBORAH NEEDLEMAN

VENDOME

NEW YORK · LONDON

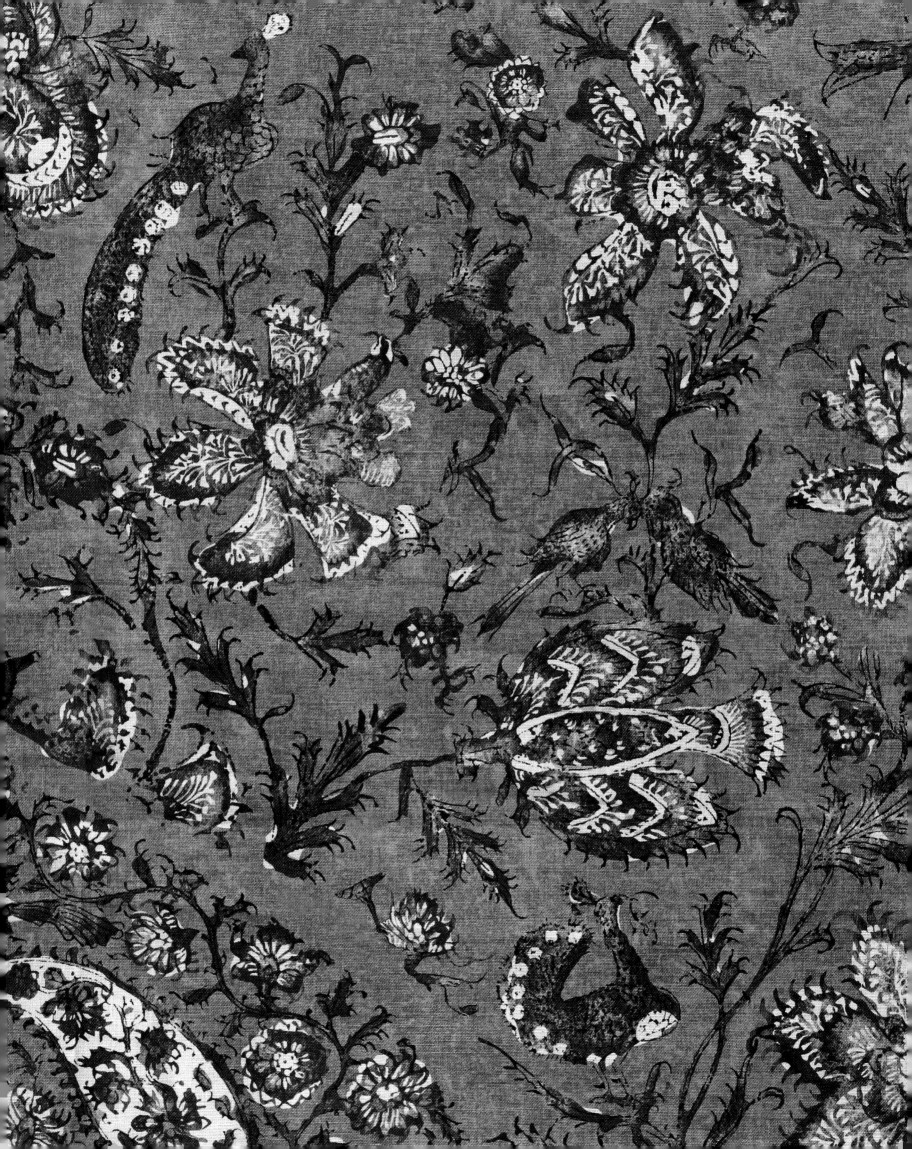

CONTENTS

FOREWORD

DEBORAH NEEDLEMAN

Lisa Fine is a wildly talented designer of rooms, clothing, and fabric, possessed of a naturally sophisticated eye for pattern and color and a masterfully light-handed way of orchestrating disparate, far-flung elements into harmony. She neither grew up immersed in design nor studied it in any professional way. And about her gifts she is entirely humble, without a lick of pretension. Were you to bring any of this up, she would most likely slough it off with a wave of her hand, leaning in instead to share, in her rapid-fire Southern drawl (a New Yorker's missile-fast, word-per-second rate paired with a Mississippian's I-have-all-the-time-in-the-world syllabic languor) some delightful tale from a recent journey or a book that has captivated her. She is excited about the wide range of marvels in the world—whether food, architecture, textiles, jewels, film, or literature—that reveal the beauty that can be wrought by other people. Lisa shares her enthusiasms so prodigiously and infectiously that it's as if they were ours too—as though we, too, were as curious and cheeky and as open to wonder as she is. In doing so, she inspires us to be so. That is the rarest of her gifts. And this book is a way for her to share it.

It is this spirit of both worldliness and generosity that animates these pages and that I hope the reader can sense in the beautifully appointed rooms that follow. The places Lisa has made and those she admires are living manifestations of their makers. A funny thing to say about rooms full of inanimate objects, but they are indeed alive. Atmosphere—invisible and yet palpable—can be elusive to capture by means of a photograph, but here Lisa is well matched by her collaborator, Miguel Flores-Vianna. He is a photographer as magnanimous and curious about the world, and as appreciative of its treasures, as she. His pictures express far more than the sum of the objects they contain.

Lisa's discovery and appreciation of the remarkable crafts of people around the world is informed by her life as an adventurer, and as a reader. Her global peregrinations have been enriched by the legacy of intrepid Western travel writers—mostly British and male, from Robert Byron and Patrick Leigh Fermor to Bruce Chatwin and Jason Elliott—who have journeyed across lands often torn apart by conflict but marked by people carrying forward their rich traditions with fortitude against a backdrop of tragedy. Damascus, Istanbul, Delhi, and Cairo are as much a part of her soul as New York, Paris, Hattiesburg, and Dallas. And indeed, it is difficult to think of Lisa without thinking of the great cultural capitals of the world, particularly those along the ancient Silk Road—from Central Asia to the Caucasus and Persia to the Middle East. It is there that economics and politics began to be interconnected across cultures—and objects traded. And it is there that the great variety of craft techniques, particularly in Lisa's beloved realm of textiles, began to spread across borders, crossbreeding and reflowering in other communities. Like the great twentieth-century architect and designer Renzo Mongiardino, Lisa sees history as continuous, an eternal present enriched by all that has come before. Her appreciation of the unique cultural heritage of places—both near and far—is backed by her support of the preservation and restoration initiatives of the World Monuments Fund and the Institute of Classical Architecture.

The paradox of the rooms Lisa makes and the textiles she designs is that they manage to feel adventurous and open to the outside world, and at the same time enveloping—complete worlds unto themselves. As a magazine editor, I have marveled at the rare way her fabrics could speak of the wonders of the world while making you feel so wonderfully cocooned and cozy. I think it is because for Lisa it is a love for the human passion embodied in things, far more than their pedigree or their arrangement, that makes her heart skip a beat—that, along with a hearty meal, a stiff drink, and a good laugh shared among friends. We may not, and most likely do not, share Lisa's innate talent, but we can share her openness to look, to learn, to be surprised, delighted, and grateful.

INTRODUCTION

During one of my first meetings with publisher Mark Magowan to discuss this book, he asked me about my childhood home in Hattiesburg, Mississippi. Haunted by this question, I began to wonder how I ever became so obsessed with design and decoration. Neither of my parents cared at all. My father's interests were books, dogs, and golf, my mother's were beauty, fashion, and travel. Things such as chintz, Louis XVI chairs, and Chinese export porcelain were never discussed.

My paternal grandmother loved gardening and silver, but any evidence of her passions were long gone by the time I was born. As the only son of a Jewish mother, my father was so grief-stricken by her death that my mother decided the only way to stop the interminable mourning was just to clear out all trace of her. A week after the funeral, my father came home to a practically empty house. The only remaining possession of his mother was an antique grandfather clock that stood on the staircase landing and loomed down as one entered the front door. I am certain it was saved only because the movers were too lazy to navigate it down the steep steps. I never found out how my father reacted to my mother's rather draconian move, but I suspect he characteristically shook his head and retreated to his room to read a good book. My father was not materialistic. When someone reported that most of my grandmother's coveted silver had been stolen by a maid, his response was, "If they take good care of my mother, they can have it." To this day I selfishly regret his magnanimity. Unlike my father, I love silver.

By the time I was born, my mother had installed wall-to-wall white carpet, black marble fireplaces, and black lacquer furniture with white cushions. The azalea bushes lining the driveway diminished bit by bit each year, and the cascades of dripping wisteria revealed more and more red brick every spring. The only evidence of my grandmother's love of gardening was a big magnolia tree in our front yard. My father's older sister Macy had planted it when she was young. I vividly remember that each year throughout my childhood the first bloom of the magnolia tree was tenderly wrapped, placed in an airfreight box, and sent to my Aunt Macy in Providence, Rhode Island.

I grew up with five dogs. Our two toy poodles and German shepherd were joined by two neighborhood strays who figured out that our house had lots of food and an open-door, dog-friendly policy. There was never a sofa or bed too precious or too clean for any or all five of the dogs to romp or wallow on at will. Once, when a horrified eighty-five-year-old great-aunt was greeted by our barking and jumping pack, my father wryly looked her in the eye and said, "They live here."

Good meals are given high priority in the South, and our house was no exception. Every day, breakfast was served at 7:30, lunch at 12:00, and dinner at 6:00. We never just grabbed a bite or wolfed something down on the run. Special occasion or not, the table was set with fine china and silver, and the food was freshly prepared with local ingredients. A creature of habit and simplicity, my father had a steak, a baked potato, green peas, and a homemade pie almost every day, while my mother, our devoted maid, Lenny, and I always ate what in the South is called "soul food": collard or mustard greens, turnips, okra, black-eyed peas, catfish . . .

OPPOSITE: A table set with a blue-and-white hand-painted ceramic plate from Laboratorio Paravicini in Milan, vintage red-and-white enamel salt and pepper holders from Aleppo, and Murano glasses from Cabana Capri. The tablecloth is Lisa Fine Textiles Kalindi in Lipstick.

ABOVE: A collection of eighteenth-century botanical watercolors is decoupaged on the walls of botanist Carl Linnaeus's bedroom at Hammarby, his estate in Sweden. OPPOSITE: An inner sanctum at l'Timad-ud-Daulah, decorated with floral painting and geometric tiles.

Everyone loved coming to our house for lunch or dinner. The food was delicious and the atmosphere was always lively and entertaining. In the pre-Walmart 1960s, grocery shopping in Mississippi was very limited, but my mother always brought French pastries, bagels, smoked salmon, and all sorts of seemingly exotic foods back from her frequent trips to New Orleans. To this day, I view every meal as an occasion, no matter how casual or formal. As Virginia Woolf wrote,

"One cannot think well, love well, sleep well, if one has not dined well."

So how did I ever become obsessed with decoration? After some reflection, I've realized that the strongest legacy from my childhood was a sense of how to live in a house. Although my parents never fussed over paint colors and fabric swatches, or pored over auction catalogues, they instilled in me an appreciation for beauty that was never contrived, and they valued

The entrance to the house of Piero Castellini in Milan. His grandfather Piero Portaluppi, an important twentieth-century Italian architect, designed the seven-sided fireplace surround and commissioned an art student in 1922 to paint the fanciful life-size botanicals and the tented ceiling. In the corner is part of the family's enormous collection of walking canes from the 1920s to the 1940s, bought from a client.

comfort over pretension. Material things are replaceable. Ambience and lifestyle flourish with curiosity, education, and pleasure. For me, without the presence of good books, delicious food, family, friends, and devoted pets, a house is not truly alive, regardless of the decoration.

In this book, I present interiors that have inspired me aesthetically. Even more inspirational are the people who live in these interiors. Not unlike my Mississippi childhood home, the interiors in this book have been created by people who love to travel, to entertain, to read, to collect, to garden. Their homes are stylistically unique in that they are a reflection of personal passions and interests that go beyond mere decorating. The creative mix of unlikely patterns, textures, and objects is the product of a curious and well-lived rich life. Flowers, Collections, and Faraway Places have always inspired me and I have organized my book thematically in that order.

✻

Although floral chintz goes in and out of fashion, I have been a steadfast believer that there is nothing prettier and fresher than a good floral anywhere, at any time of year. Many of my

The pergola-covered alfresco dining room in the garden of interior designer Katie Ridder and her husband, architect Peter Pennoyer, at their home in Millbrook, New York.

textile designs are florals inspired by botanical paintings, Indian block prints, batiks, and eighteenth-century chintzes, some dating back to the original cotton chintz made in India for the European markets. Flowers, whether in the garden, in a vase, in a print, upholstered on walls and furniture, or hand painted on porcelain or a mural lift my spirits.

I love the feeling of rooms that are so alive with flowers and nature's colors that you almost feel as though you are outdoors. One of the most beautiful examples of this is seen in the bedroom of the acclaimed eighteenth-century botanist Carl Linnaeus at Hammarby, his estate in Sweden. He covered the walls with original botanical watercolors; they were the first thing he would see when he awoke each morning and the last thing he'd see when he went to bed each night. Although Linnaeus's primary interest was in the magic of nature, his botanical decoupage inspired designers worldwide and has been re-created and reinterpreted countless times and in myriad ways. I also love interiors that naturally flow into gardens, such as interior designer Katie Ridder's garden in Millbrook, New York, with its pergola-covered, open-air dining room, as if the garden were an extension of the house itself.

In the process of looking to artistic interpretations of flowers and animals for my own designs, I have grown to love the gardens that inspired the art. What I wouldn't give to see an original Persian garden! I have studied innumerable images of birds, roses, deer, peacocks, and pomegranate and citrus trees in Persian gardens as rendered in paintings, rugs, antique textiles, and inlaid furniture in an attempt to capture their elusive beauty. Perhaps that is why the garden at the tomb of l'Timad-ud-Daulah in Agra is one of my favorite places. It is often referred to as the "Baby Taj" or the "Little Jewel." Although the original garden no longer exists, the World Monuments Fund has worked to restore it as faithfully as possible. The interior wall paintings of the mausoleum are covered with depictions of intricate florals combined with stylized arabesque and geometric patterns, culminating in the most elaborately ornamented honeycomb ceiling. The magnificence inside and out reflects the importance of nature and the garden in Mughal culture.

✿

Many collections begin with the love of an object or objects, or something that just speaks to you. I am drawn to the rich colors and patterns found in Indian and Persian miniature paintings and textiles. Whenever I am in Delhi, I carve out an entire morning or afternoon to visit with Chhotelal Bharany and listen, entranced, as he shares stories about many of the precious textiles in his world-renowned collection. I always leave seeing color and pattern differently. His enthusiasm is infectious, especially when he is holding one of his rare Kashmir shawls and declares, "I can't believe the human hand can make this; it is the work of God."

I also love idiosyncratic collections, such as those in the Milan family home of Piero Castellini. Everything from taxidermy, tortoiseshells, and sawfish to eighteenth- and nineteenth-century gouaches of Naples and Mt. Vesuvius and Greek and Roman antiquities covers walls and surfaces. The members of each generation have been obsessive collectors, creating a layering of curiosities so magical that you feel transplanted to a world of fantasy the minute you step foot into the trompe l'oeil winter garden room, an

entrance painted with a series of botanical studies and a faux-tented ceiling.

Although each collector is different, all are passionate about whatever they collect. The collections featured in the book range widely over space and time, and they not only reflect the collectors' personalities but also impart a unique charm to their homes. Every one of them cherishes the rarity and beauty of the individual objects, whether a seashell found on the beach or a priceless sculpture bought at auction. To quote designer Rose Tarlow, "People who collect out of love are exempt from the dictates that govern traditional design, for there are no rules for lovers. Passionate collectors often give their houses an enchanted quality."

✿

I am also inspired by people who become obsessed with faraway places and cultures. Long before I visited a foreign country, I was infatuated with the British writer, adventuress, and *Vogue* editor Lesley Blanch. Her books *The Wilder Shores of Love* and *The Sabres of Paradise* captured the romanticism of exotic lands, stirring her readers' imagination about the world of harems and tents in the Middle East and the Caucasus. Always fearless and curious, Blanch took every opportunity to catch a bus, a train, a plane, a boat, or even a mule to explore the most remote, often uninhabited, destinations. Although she lived much of her life in England and France, her homes always reflected her travels. Russian icons, tribal embroidery, and Turkish rugs were some of her favorite treasures. She wore caftans, turbans, stacks of bangles, and layers of necklaces. She essentially brought her adventures home to the South of France, where she died at age 103. The last section of the book focuses on the interiors of people who have embraced the aesthetics of distant cultures and seamlessly incorporate them into their own worlds.

The faraway place that has most inspired me is India. It is a place you must see, smell, and touch to grasp the intensity, the contradictions, the chaos, and most importantly, the indescribable beauty. Nothing you read or hear can fully prepare you for such an explosion of the senses. Most people either love India or hate it. I first went there to create special

OPPOSITE: A collection of eighteenth- and nineteenth-century paintings of Mt. Vesuvius erupting hangs above stacks of striped shirts in Castellini's dressing room. Castellini has a fetish for striped shirts; he hoards them!

embroideries, then to work with block printers, then to produce embroidered blouses and coats for Irving & Fine. Over the past twenty years I have met many designers and writers who, like me, have found inspiration there.

My introduction to India was in the downtown Manhattan apartment of Los Angeles decorator Peter Dunham. Peter had transformed a tiny, nondescript space into an exotic den that only someone who has traveled the world extensively could create. Every inch of the room was covered or draped with layers of prints and embroideries, all made in India or in one of those remote "Stan" countries I was not yet familiar with. A large ivory architectural model of the Taj Mahal sat on top of an antique suzani next to the sofa. There was no color scheme, no plan; everything seemed to have just fallen into "its" place. I once read that the Italian architect and designer Renzo Mongiardino said, "A room should sing and dance." This room did. Although it was another ten years before I visited India for the first time, I will always credit Peter for having opened my eyes to the country that became my greatest source of inspiration.

I was living in Paris, working as a contributing editor for Marian McEvoy at *Elle Decor*, when I met Miguel Flores-Vianna, the photographer of this book, for the first time. Within a week of our meeting, we found ourselves working together on a magazine story in Cadaqués, Spain. I knew then that Miguel would be a friend and an inspiration for life. Driven by an insatiable curiosity and an intrepid spirit, Miguel lives to explore and discover. He finds beauty in the humble and in the sumptuous. A couple of summers ago, while sharing photographs of travels and interiors during breakfast in a London café, Miguel and I conceived the idea for this book. *Near & Far* is a collection of interiors I love, captured by the lens of one of the most gifted people I have ever been lucky enough to know.

OPPOSITE: A rare book on Indian block prints from the Calico Museum of Textiles in Ahmedabad lies next to an urn from Galerie J. Kugel in Paris. ABOVE: A Persian illustration of a pomegranate tree from the thirteenth-century cosmography *'Ajā'ib al-makhluqāt wa ghara'ib al-mawjūdāt* by Zakariya al-Qazwini.

FLOWERS

AT HOME IN DALLAS

When I was helping my mother decorate her Dallas apartment, I decided to revert to a Southern tradition of spring/summer chintz slipcovers. I slipcovered the entire living room in a peacock-blue and apple-green cabbage rose chintz from my textile collection. We liked it so much that we decided to leave it year round.

The Pasha fabric in my Dallas bedroom was inspired by the flora and fauna found in the border of a Persian miniature painting and by the palm trees in a palampore from the Calico Museum of Textiles in Ahmedabad, India. I particularly love the combination of this imaginary Mughal garden with the colorful, naïve paintings by Calcutta-based artist Sunita Kumar, a close friend of Mother Teresa.

One of my favorite finds is a sculpture of broken blue-and-white Chinese export porcelain that was discovered at the bottom of the ocean three hundred years after a Dutch East India Company ship was lost at sea. The sculpture was created not by an artist's hand but by a shipwreck. This piece was among crates upon crates of Chinese export porcelain that Dallas collector Betty Gertz and Antwerp tastemaker Axel Vervoordt bought at Christie's Amsterdam in 1984 from the auction of the Hatcher Cargo Collection. Although the flowers are no longer clearly visible, the beauty of the hand painting is still detectable in traces of leaves and blossoms. A large piece of coral protrudes upward as if growing from the shards of the broken plates.

PAGE 20: Lisa Fine Textiles Arabella in Peacock/Apple, printed on 100 percent cotton.

PAGE 21: In the living room, GoGo, my Bedlington Terrier, rests on a sofa in front of a black-lacquered screen from my childhood home in Mississippi. My uncle shipped it from China in the 1950s.

PAGES 22–23: In a long, gallery-like space, two seating areas flank the dining area. The large, low, black-lacquered table was designed by Jeffrey Bilhuber as both a coffee table and an ottoman. Another ottoman is covered in a hand-woven wool bedcover from India, bought at Hollywood at Home in Los Angeles. The broken Chinese export sculpture from the famous Hatcher Cargo Collection was found at Fremontier Antiquaires on Paris's Left Bank.

PAGE 24: The twentieth-century camel ceramic garden stool is from Nick Brock Antiques in Dallas.

PAGE 25: A nineteenth-century Chinese pagoda, spotted by interior designer Tom Scheerer, is also from Nick Brock Antiques. Tom insisted that I acquire it, saying that the room wouldn't be complete until the pagoda was in place.

PAGE 26: In the dining area, the Frances Elkins cream-lacquered Loop chairs were found and purchased by New York interior designer Richard Keith Langham from the shoe department at Gus Mayer in Birmingham, Alabama. The blue-and-white Delft centerpieces are from Nick Brock Antiques.

PAGE 27: Lisa Fine Textiles Konkan in Ocean Blue, printed on 100 percent linen, serves as a tablecloth. The china is Richard Ginori's Oriente Italiano Azalea pattern. The hand-blown green glasses with a sapphire-blue border are from Giberto in Venice. I acquired the silver oyster-shell salt and pepper holders at the Sotheby's Paris auction of Madeleine Castaing's estate.

PAGES 28–29: The collection of small, hand-blown colored-glass vases is from Dallas friend Sissy Cullum. The large, hand-blown water glasses are from LagunaB in Venice. I found the hand-painted Iznik plates in Istanbul.

PAGE 30: De Gournay's hand-painted wallpaper of the Indus River Valley is an appropriate theme for the entrance to an apartment filled with influences near and far. A bench inlaid with bone from Samurai Exports in Jaipur is covered in an ikat velvet from Seref Ozen in Istanbul. It sits atop an orange Ushak from Abrash Rug Gallery in Dallas.

PAGE 31: Among the series of Indian miniature paintings is a scene of a tiger hunt from the Kasliwal family's Gem Palace in Jaipur.

PAGES 32–33: The walls of this cozy sitting room are upholstered in Lisa Fine Textiles Malula in Coco. All of the Indian miniatures and portraits, collected over the years, are framed in camel bone. Most of them were found in New Delhi.

PAGES 34–35: The master bedroom's walls are upholstered in Lisa Fine Textiles Pandora in Terra Cotta, printed on linen. The marble tassel column lamps were found at Again & Again in Dallas. The lampshades, made by Cele Johnson in Dallas, are Lisa Fine Textiles Jaisalmer in Jaipur Pink. The collage over the bed is by London-based Iranian artist Afsoon. It depicts a scene from the *Shahnameh*, the epic poem written by Ferdowsi between ca. 977 and 1010.

PAGE 36: The walls in my bedroom are upholstered in Lisa Fine Textiles Pasha in Monsoon Blue, printed on linen. The paintings of Mother Teresa, Gandhi, and a sacred cow are by Calcutta artist Sunita Kumar, a dear friend of Mother Teresa. I fell in love with them when I visited Kumar in her Calcutta home.

PENNY MORRISON

WALES

The bucolic estate of London-based interior designer Penny Morrison and her husband, Guy, in Wales is the quintessential country house. In spring and summer, every room on the ground floor opens to one of the many terraces or gardens. In winter, a fire blazes in every room. Penny fills the house with bouquets of flowers from her walled garden or wildflowers from the fields. "A room is not alive without fresh flowers," she insists.

Inside, floral prints abound. Her own prints, Penny Morrison Textiles, mix with embroideries of oversized tulips or leafy vines from Turkey and carnation-strewn suzanis. In one of the bedrooms, a tree of life pattern covers the walls and a cabbage rose Bessarabian rug lies at the foot of a bed adorned with a tonal, carnation-stripe canopy. In the kitchen and breakfast room, the cupboards and shelves display a collection of ceramics and porcelain, many featuring bouquets of flowers or landscape scenes. Her dining room chairs are upholstered with a

multicolored palm-frond print. Whether fresh, printed, painted, or embroidered, the flowers have no common theme, color, or origin. Instinctively, Penny assembles a colorful world rampant with patterns, all inspired by nature and travel.

The Morrisons embrace the old-fashioned country-house tradition of spoiling their guests. Visitors typically arrive on Friday evening for cocktails on one of the terraces, followed by dinner, which often lasts past midnight. In summer, lunches are usually served outside in one of the gardens or on a terrace facing a garden or a field of wildflowers.

Before guests arrive, fresh flowers are placed in every bedroom and a strict protocol is observed: white bed linens and towels, down pillows, a fluffy white terrycloth robe for every guest in winter, a white cotton waffle robe in summer, and a hot water bottle between the sheets each night.

Penny's personality, like her house, is big and bold, yet warm and cozy, and exudes creativity.

PAGE 38: Lisa Fine Textile Noor in Indigo.

PAGE 39: In the drawing room, a painting by George Harcourt, *The Crypt at St. Martin's*, hangs over an antique, marble-topped, painted table found at an antiques shop on Pimlico Road in London. The square cachepots faced with antique tiles are Swedish.

PAGES 40–41: A view from one of the many terraces of the lush rolling hills dotted with sheep in the bucolic Welsh countryside.

PAGES 42–43: On the console in the entrance hall are a pair of antique geese acquired at Christie's and a pair of lamps with custom-made shades from Penny Morrison Accessories. The plaster busts on marble stands are also from Christie's. The rug is from the Moroccan town of Asilah, just south of Tangier.

PAGES 44–45: In the formal living room, a pair of French gilt chairs and two upholstered sofas surround a suzani-covered ottoman, where Petal, the Morrisons' Labrador, relaxes. The walls are covered with a collection of silhouettes, portraits, and landscapes. A collection of blue-and-white Delft and English porcelain is displayed on a demilune table. Wherever she happens to be, Penny spends every weekend combing markets and shops.

PAGE 46: A Tod Ramos painting of the Cheltenham Races dominates this corner of the library.

PAGE 47: A watercolor of a duck by eighteenth-century British artist Peter Paillou fronts the bookshelves in the library. The brass lamp on a side table has a custom-made shade from Penny Morrison Accessories.

PAGES 48–49: The library's French doors open onto the park-like grounds. The room is full of vibrant colors and patterns. The walls, painted in Farrow & Ball's Arsenic Green, are in striking contrast to the red-and-white curtains in Penny Morrison's Arabella print.

PAGES 50–51: The shelves in the breakfast room display Penny's collection of ceramics, acquired over the years from country antiques fairs and shops. Those on the table are filled with sweet peas from the garden. The walls and the table are painted in a mix of Farrow & Ball's Pigeon and Light Blue.

PAGE 52: The open shelving in the kitchen displays a collection of antique French faience plates, English bowls, and French enamel canisters. The chairs are covered in Penny Morrison's Gobi Blue print, and the tablecloth is Gobi Red on Blue.

PAGE 53: The deer heads mounted on the wall of the stairwell came with the house when the Morrisons bought it. The painting of deer is by nineteenth-century English artist Samuel Carter.

PAGE 54: A guest bedroom is lined with Penny Morrison's Begum wallpaper. Underfoot is a nineteenth-century Bessarabian floral rug. The ivory damask curtains are trimmed in Colefax and Fowler fan edging.

PAGE 55: The silver mirror and set of brushes on the dressing table were inherited from Guy's grandfather. The green ikat covering the table is from Carolina Irving Textiles.

PAGES 56–57: In this guest bedroom, the bed hangings and armchair slipcover are Penny Morrison's Pasha print.

PAGES 58–59: The Regency house is located 180 miles from central London, just over the Welsh border. The long, winding drive is lined with ball-shaped boxwood shrubs, which the Morrisons planted thirty years ago, when they purchased the house.

PAGE 60: A large cherry tree is surrounded by wildflowers. The Regency bench is original to the property.

SARAH GRAHAM

LONDON

Scottish artist Sarah Graham has always been obsessed by the natural world. As a child, she voraciously studied the plants and insects found on the pages of her family's extensive collection of seventeenth- and eighteenth-century horticultural and entomological books. Her favorite outings were trips to Harrod's pet department, where she bought mice to feed her father's pet carpet python, which resided in his office at the House of Lords. Today, when Graham is not in her studio surrounded by her collection of skulls, fossils, butterflies, and other insects, she can often be found at the Viktor Wynd Museum of Curiosities in London's Hackney neighborhood or poring over the entomology archives in London's Natural History Museum.

Graham does not like it when her work is described as pretty. She prefers masculine, sculptural, sensual, strong. In her drawings and paintings, putatively ugly insects become beautiful and delicate flowers are never feminine. Just like her subjects, everything about Graham's art is natural. The rich, saturated colors are created from organic matter—brown from birch wood, purple from elderberries, green from dyer's broom, sepia from cuttlefish—and mixed with pure graphite to make inks. Everything is drawn and painted freehand on handmade calligraphy paper. Once the ink touches the paper, it is there to stay. Every dribble or blot becomes part of the finished product. The imperfections are part of the magnificence.

PAGE 62: Lisa Fine Textiles Tika in Lilac.

PAGE 63: Graham's paintings of her signature flower, amaryllis, illustrate the enormous and powerful scale of her work.

PAGE 64: A very large charcoal sketch of an amaryllis serves as a study for the ink version.

PAGE 65: An assortment of objects from the natural world—fossils, shells, nuts, dried flowers—sits next to a sketchbook of Graham's drawings of her observations.

PAGES 66–67: An overview of Graham's studio.

PAGES 68–69: Graham describes her work as strong and sculptural.

PAGES 70–71: A cabinet is filled with books on horticulture and entomology, a collection of mounted butterflies and other insects, and animal skeletons and skulls.

PAGE 72: A model specimen of a *Magnolia grandiflora* rests in front of two mounted insects, a giant leaf-eating mantis and an African horned beetle.

SVINDERSVIK

SWEDEN

On a recent trip to Sweden with the Institute of Classical Architecture, I saw traces of the Swedish East India Company's influence everywhere I went—in auction houses, palaces, and manor houses. One of the highlights was the eighteenth-century French-inspired Rococo manor house Svindersvik, built in the 1740s by Swedish architect Carl Hårleman, who was also responsible for the interiors of Stockholm's enormous royal palace.

Commissioned by Claes Grill, the director of the Swedish East India Company at the time, Svindersvik is but a short distance from Stockholm—a quick boat trip in Grill's day. The original hand-painted Chinese rice wallpaper with flower and bird motifs is still in place in the antechamber, as is the original collection of gilded Rococo furniture. The walls of the master bedroom are covered in a colorful floral paper, also from China. Even the tiled stoves have a Chinese floral pattern. It seems that wherever I travel, I derive inspiration from flowers.

PAGE 74: Lisa Fine Textiles Paradeiza in Sky Blue.

PAGE 75: A detail of the eighteenth-century hand-painted rice wallpaper brought to Sweden from China by the Swedish East India Company.

PAGES 76–77: In the antechamber, the eighteenth-century gilt mirrors and clock and the silk damask slipcovers are typical of the French Rococo style.

PAGES 78–79: Unlike the exuberant antechamber, the dining room is decorated in a more sober, classical vein.

PAGES 80–81: In the master bedroom, the lively floral Chinese wallpaper is charmingly offset by cotton gingham upholstery and curtains.

PAGES 82–83: The interior of a separate party pavilion dates to a slightly later period, and the painted walls feature Ionic columns, medallions, garlands, birds, and antique figures—all hallmarks of Gustavian decoration.

PAGE 84: A perfect example of Svindersvik's mix of Swedish Rococo furniture, Chinese floral wallpaper, blue-and-white-tiled stove, and cotton gingham upholstery

CHARLOTTE MOSS

NEW YORK

Charlotte Moss is a force of nature—a voracious reader, a passionate gardener, the ultimate hostess, a renowned interior designer, a philanthropist, and the author of ten books. The list of her accomplishments, awards, and interests is much too long to enumerate. However, it is her insatiable curiosity, unbounded generosity, and sense of adventure that I cherish most.

Her love of history and her tenacity impressed the Thomas Jefferson Foundation when she spearheaded the fundraising to restore the dining room at Monticello to its original color after it was discovered that in Jefferson's day the room was yellow, not Wedgwood blue. Such details matter to Charlotte. Her art and design connoisseurship is seen throughout both her East Hampton house and her Manhattan townhouse. Each piece of furniture tells a story, whether it is a garden table that once belonged to Bunny Mellon, Evangeline

Bruce's canopy bed, or an offering cup from a black Baptist church in Virginia.

The floral batiks and cabbage rose chintzes throughout both houses enhance the Old World charm and comfort that are signatures of Charlotte's interiors. In the main sitting room in East Hampton, a pair of large French jardinières with potted palms direct your eye toward the gardens outside, where Charlotte loves to spend as much time as possible. She confesses that working in the garden and potting room is her therapy.

Whether Charlotte is entertaining houseguests, planning a luncheon or dinner party, or simply relaxing at home with her husband, Barry, she treats every day as an occasion. Although everything in Charlotte's world seems effortless, nothing is incidental. She is a perfectionist by nature, and her houses and gardens continually evolve because she never stops studying and creating.

KARL LAGERFELD   VILLA NOAILLES HYÈRES—ÉTÉ 1990   STEIDL

The Bedroom

CASSELL'S EUROPEAN FERNS

PAGE 86: Lisa Fine Textiles Jaisalmer in Tobacco.

PAGE 87: The painting above the fireplace in the library of her New York townhouse is *Unraveled* by Louise Fenne from Ann Long Fine Art in Charleston, South Carolina. The walls are covered in a tomato-red gauffrage from Pierre Frey and the custom-made carpet is also from Pierre Frey.

PAGES 88–89: A collection of paintings and watercolors of interiors by Walter Gay, Benjamin William Latrobe, William Ellis Rankin, Cecil Beaton, Pierre Bergian, Hugh Buchanan, and others adorns a wall between the bookcases in the library.

PAGES 90–91: The walls of the living room were striéd by James Alan Smith, The small settee is upholstered in a fabric by Sabina Fay Braxton. The painting is by Paul César Helleu.

PAGES 92–93: Charlotte's home office, on the top floor of her Manhattan townhouse, is devoted to design inspiration and study. The facing desks were custom made by Tony Victoria of Victoria & Son, and the curtains are a Braquenié fabric. The walls are covered with a collection of fashion and design photographs and illustrations by Man Ray, Horst, Lillian Bassman, Cecil Beaton, Gloria Vanderbilt, Andy Warhol, Ruben Toledo, and many others.

PAGES 94–95: In the sitting room of Charlotte's East Hampton house, a pair of faux-marble Italian columns holds a pair of French jardinières. A Louis XV chaise is upholstered in her Digby Tent pattern for Brunschwig & Fils.

PAGE 96: A collection of ceramic and glass vases filled with roses and other blooms from her garden sit on an Indian block-print tablecloth from Simrane in Paris.

PAGE 97: Wicker baskets of all shapes and sizes hang from the ceiling of Charlotte's potting room.

PAGES 98–99: The shelves in the potting room display a great variety of Delft, English porcelain, and creamware vases, urns, and tulipieres.

PAGES 100–101: In the New York master bedroom, watercolors from the estate of William Paley hang above a pair of opaline cachepots from the estate of Madeleine Castaing. The wall fabric is by Claremont, and the embroidery on the headboard is a classical nineteenth-century pattern adapted by Penn & Fletcher.

PAGES 102–3: A pair of black-lacquered chinoiserie four-poster twin beds found at auction and black-lacquered screen panels converted into closet doors were the inspiration for this Orientalist guest room. The tole clematis on the mantel is by New York artist Vladimir Kanevsky.

PAGE 104: A tole apple branch with a butterfly by Carmen Almon rests on a black-lacquered chinoiserie table by Jansen.

PAGE 105: An ivory paper knife sits next to an open book of botanicals on Charlotte's desk in East Hampton.

PAGE 106: An eighteenth-century black-lacquered secretary holds an easel displaying a Delacroix sketch of a Moroccan scene. The desk chair is from the estate of Evangeline Bruce, and the eighteenth-century Italian chair is from the estate of Lilian Gish.

CHRISTOPHER MOORE

NEW DEHLI

I first discovered Christopher Moore on Instagram. Mesmerized by each post of French provincial floral prints, one more beautiful than the next, I was determined to meet this enigmatic figure. Every time I went to Delhi I contacted him in advance, and every time the elusive Mr. Moore was otherwise engaged.

Moore, better known as "The Toileman," was famous in design circles for his London shop, specializing in antique toiles de Jouy. But after a trip to India in 1998, his life changed. He fell in love with both the country and its textiles, and decided to set up a home and a textile-printing company there.

Moore has mastered "the Indian textile that is not Indian." On the top floor of his house in Noida, outside Delhi, is his archive—a treasure trove of textiles. Many are eighteenth- and nineteenth-century European florals inspired by the original seventeenth-century Indian chintzes made for the European market. All are colored with vegetable dyes, including rich madder reds, indigos, saffrons, and tobaccos. Scattered among the stacks of antique quilts and vintage costumes are strike-offs from his own Christopher Moore Collection.

When I finally managed to visit Moore, every textile I admired prompted a story that inevitably led to another story. For example, when Prince Charles complimented the fabric that Moore had used for the curtains in the dining room of the British embassy in Delhi, a custom order for the Castle of Mey in Scotland soon followed. Then there was the tale of the bulletproof curtains Moore made for the British embassy in Afghanistan. His stories are almost as colorful and captivating as his textiles.

N.º 1303

N.º 1304

N.º 1306.

N.º 1308.

N.º 1309

N.º 1056

Nº 1311.

2486

Nº 20.

Nº 1316.

Nº 1315.

PAGE 108: Lisa Fine Textiles Kashgar in Spice.

PAGE 109: A bowl of fresh lotus blossoms from the street vendor down the road adorn a handmade resist-dyed indigo tablecloth.

PAGE 110: A detail of one of the innumerable textiles in Moore's archive.

PAGE 111: In Moore's pink sitting/dining room, the table is covered with his Applegate floral print, the curtains are his Arcadia, and the sofa is upholstered in his striped fabric Boucher.

PAGES 112–13: The furniture in the sitting/dining room is covered in prints from Moore's collection, including, stripes, florals, indigo batiks, and resist-dyed fabrics. Like the dining table, the pillows and chairs are covered in in Applegate.

PAGES 114–15: An original sample book from a textile manufacturer, probably the French firm Oberkampf, one of many in Moore's archive.

PAGES 116–17: A cabinet in Moore's archive is filled with a collection of eighteenth- and nineteenth-century quilts and costumes in cotton floral prints and stripes with natural dyes.

PAGE 118: Moore's favorite indigo, which was custom printed for the Castle of Mey in Scotland at the request of Prince Charles.

COLLECTIONS

AT HOME IN NEW YORK

After spending more than ten years shut-tling between New York and Paris, I decided I wanted to live in New York full time. The downside of this decision was abandoning a charming Old World apartment on rue de Lille for an apartment in an unremarkable 1960s building on Third Avenue. In Paris, all the rooms had big French doors and windows facing an ivy-covered courtyard. Now I have a view of a bank branch and an Italian restaurant. Instead of graceful rooms with elegant proportions, I have box-like rooms with institutional proportions.

To mask the architectural blandness and low ceilings, I lined every wall and some of the ceilings in linen and covered the floors in handwoven raffia matting. For the bedrooms, I chose two of my tex-tiles, Mughal Flower and Samode, both featuring repeats of a simple, single Indian flower. And for the living room, I went with a subtle, paper-backed chevron stripe. I love the cocoon effect that wrap-ping a room in one beautiful print creates.

For the living room I chose natural colors—golden sand and straw—and I slipcovered the red velvet banquettes from my Paris apartment in a creamy hemp. Even before I started decorating the room, I was surprised by how much I liked this linen-and-raffia box. The atmosphere was sooth-ing, almost like an Asian spa, and the texture of the natural fabrics created a perfect foundation for the color to follow: pillows made from Kashmir shawls, Moroccan embroideries, Turkish velvets, and Indian block prints, along with black-lacquered pieces and French and Italian chairs. In the end, the result was anything but bland or colorless.

One of my favorite pieces in my New York apartment is a gilded carved-wood and stucco mir-ror that I found in a secondhand shop in an Istanbul market. I was traveling with Jamie Creel and Marco Scarani when I spotted it propped up against a back wall behind layers of dusty junk. It was so long ago that it took all three of us two days to withdraw enough cash from ATMs to purchase it. Needless to say, Jamie and Marco were not happy with me, but I was not leaving Turkey without it. The following summer, while visiting an old Ottoman palace in Damascus, I was astonished to see that the ballroom was lined with the exact same mirrors. Whether my mirror is valuable or not, whether it came from a junk shop or an Ottoman palace, is irrelevant; what matters is that it spoke to me.

A PASSIONATE EYE
A HOUSE IN THE COUNTRY
MAHARAJA
GREAT HOUSES
Damascus Tiles

PAGE 122: Lisa Fine Textiles Rambagh Reverse in Curry.

PAGE 123: The living room walls are covered in Lisa Fine Textiles Luxor in Sand, printed on paper-backed linen. The large, hand-sculpted ceramic casserole dish from Ardmore in South Africa serving as a planter was a gift from Jamie Creel of Creel and Gow. The painting of the Bedlington Terrier, found in an antiques store in the English country-side, was a gift from Carol Mack. The small silver tray with an engraved peacock was a gift from Charlotte Moss. The large faux-tortoiseshell mirror is from John Rosselli & Associates. The Irish-style console was designed by Penny Morrison.

PAGES 124–25: I slipcovered the red velvet banquettes from my Paris apartment in natural hemp from Libeco in Belgium. The gilded carved-wood and stucco mirror, originally from Syria, was found in an Istanbul market. The top two drawings flanking it are sketches of heaven and hell by Bernard Boutet de Monvel from Christie's Paris, a gift from Jack Swain. In the middle to the left of the mirror is a Company School miniature of a Calcutta house from Martyn Gregory in London. The black-lacquered coffee table is part of the Baker Far East Collection by Michael Taylor from the 1950s, found at Again & Again in Dallas.

PAGE 126: The large photograph of the synagogue in Cochin, India, is part of Karen Knorr's *India Song* series from Danziger Gallery in New York. The black-lacquered drum is one of a pair from Nick Brock Antiques in Dallas. The two French chairs are from the Marché aux Puces in Paris and are covered in a velvet ikat from Seref Ozen in Istanbul.

PAGE 127: The unfinished oil painting of a camel is a study by Boutet de Monvel for one of his Moroccan paintings. The Delft vases are from Bardith in New York.

PAGES 128–29: In the dining area of the living room, the table is set with nineteenth-century Meissen l'Inde china, glasses from Moleria Locchi in Florence and LagunaB in Venice, and bamboo flatware from Neiman Marcus. The gilded stork candlesticks are from Kenneth Neame Antiques & Interior Decorations in London. The eighteenth-century Italian chairs are from R. Louis Bofferding in New York and came from the estate of Whitney Warren Jr. of San Francisco.

PAGE 130: The walls and ceiling of the guest bedroom are covered in Lisa Fine Textiles Samode in Pompeii, printed on paper-backed linen. The carved-wood camel table was found at Flore de Brantes's Flore Art Gallery in Brussels. The inlaid chest is from Tangier, and the bright orange pillow with hot pink embroidery is a nineteenth-century textile remnant found at Bharany in New Delhi.

PAGE 131: The elephant paintings were entries in a painting competition in Udaipur. The saffron wool bedcover with white embroidery is from Andraab in India. The green-lacquered bed tray was designed by Jeffrey Bilhuber for KRB in New York. The pillows are from Good Earth at Khan Market in New Delhi.

PAGES 132–33: The walls and ceiling of my bedroom are upholstered in Lisa Fine Textiles Mughal Flower in Rose, printed on 100 percent linen. The king-size, hammered-silver four-poster bed comes from Samurai Exports in Jaipur. The headboard was custom embroidered in India, and the lampshades were made by Blanche P. Field in New York out of silk Indian saris.

PAGE 134: The vintage blue-and-pink-striped dhurrie was made in the Bikaner jail and found at Samurai Exports in Jaipur. The pink lamps were found on the Dixie Highway in Miami, and the lampshades were also made out of silk saris by Blanche P. Field.

CHARLOTTE AND ALEXANDER DI CARCACI

LONDON

It's not surprising that Charlotte and Alexander di Carcaci live only in seventeenth- or eighteenth-century houses. The first time I met Charlotte, she appeared like a vision floating across the old-fashioned tea room at Brown's Hotel in London. When I remarked that she looked like one of the aristocratic beauties in a Romney portrait, she blushed and confessed that Romney had, in fact, painted several of her family's portraits.

Charlotte is quintessentially English. Alex is Sicilian and resembles someone who would be more at home in a ballroom scene in Visconti's film *The Leopard* than on Cheyne Row or in Richmond, where they live. Whenever I'm in London, we visit stately historical houses, and I am always astounded by their encyclopedic knowledge of history, painting, and the decorative arts. To witness them discover and discuss a new-found treasure confirms how deeply rooted they are in a rarified world of aesthetics.

Charlotte and Alex have the cultivated eye that distinguishes true collectors, but they are not restricted by time or place; nor are they susceptible to passing trends and fashions. In taste and personality, they are truly original. In Alex's antiques shop, Carcaci/McWhirter, he mixes Delft vases, majolica from Seville, and Qajar tiles with important eighteenth-century pieces found all over Europe, many from private collections and homes.

The di Carcacis' house reflects the refined taste of their backgrounds, yet the décor is effortlessly casual, and the atmosphere is bohemian with a touch of the eccentric. In the sitting room, an oil of Zeus, Venus, and Cupid painted in the Veneto in about 1520 hangs next to eighteenth-century garden prints and across from a portrait of Alex's grandmother painted by John da Costa, ca. 1915. A small wooden Turkish table from Peter Hinwood adds a touch of exoticism. The furniture is upholstered in simple and classic cotton stripes, ginghams, or paisleys.

PAGE 136: Lisa Fine Textiles Konkan in Ocean Blue.

PAGE 137: An eighteenth-century hand-painted Northern Italian bureau and bookcase.

PAGE 138: A portrait of Alex's grandmother, painted by John da Costa, ca. 1915, hangs next to the fireplace, where an early eighteenth-century overmantel mirror reflects the English eighteenth-century prints across the room. A green, tile-topped Moroccan table bought from Peter Hinwood sits next to an armchair covered in a pink-and-white gingham from Ian Mankin in London.

PAGE 139: An early sixteenth-century painting of Zeus, Venus, and Cupid is surrounded by eighteenth-century English garden prints. Charlie, a rescue dog found on the streets of Patmos, is sleeping on the pink-and-white gingham sofa.

PAGE 140: In the dining room, a portrait of Alex's grandfather Francesco Paternò Castello di Carcaci, painted in Florence in 1925, hangs next to a niche filled with an assortment of blue-and-white vases, Qajar tiles, and a collection of 1920s Italian silver plates.

PAGE 141: The original eighteenth-century paneling is extant all over the house. The mahogany dining chairs are mid-eighteenth-century English.

PAGE 142: The walls in the standalone studio in the di Carcacis' garden are painted in Sanderson's Pink Allure. Dominating the room is a Mughal portrait of the Maharaja of Udaipur, bought from James McWhirter. The brown-and-white-cotton paisley print on the sofa is vintage John Stefanidis.

PAGE 143: An eighteenth-century Italian chair, covered in a favorite pink-and-white stripe, holds an Indian miniature.

PAGE 144: Cotton prints from Rajasthan serve as bedcoverings for a pair of four-poster twin beds from Habitat.

PAGE 145: An English eighteenth-century print of two Regency ladies with exaggeratedly tall wigs adorned with plumes.

PAGE 146: Blue-and-white eighteenth- and nineteenth-century vases are grouped in front of a red-and-white silk textile fragment woven for the Maréchal de Saxe, Louis XV's great military leader. The tiles were made in Seville in the mid-sixteenth century.

ALEXIS AND NICOLAS KUGEL

PARIS

When I first moved to Paris, the New York–based French interior designer Robert Couturier invited me to dinner at Anahi, an Argentine steakhouse, where I met Natalie and Nicolas Kugel. That night was the beginning of a long friendship and an invaluable education in a rarified world of collecting.

Some of my most memorable days in Paris were spent at the Galerie J. Kugel, located in the elegant neoclassical Hôtel Collot on quai Anatole France. The brothers Alexis and Nicolas Kugel are fifth-generation dealers who preside over a world-renowned collection of masterpieces dating from 500 B.C. to the mid-nineteenth century. The Kugels specialize in rare, often eclectic, and always authentic objects and paintings. When a journalist asked Alex if he was concerned that antiques were out of fashion, he smiled and responded, "Not at all; now they are left for passionate collectors."

Among their many collections is a menagerie of gilded-bronze animal-shaped automaton clocks, made in Renaissance Augsburg, Germany, and often given as gifts to Chinese emperors and European kings. This "Mechanical Bestiary," consisting of camels, elephants, monkeys, lions, and bears, most accompanied by trainers or Nubian attendants, is the largest and rarest of its kind. Only the Kugel brothers would have thought to host our mutual friend George Farias's sixtieth birthday party in their gallery with these treasures as centerpieces.

But even more memorable for me was the day Nicolas showed me a small marble urn with stylized pearl ornamentation. Heartbroken, I had just put my fifteen-year-old Wheaten Terrier Malula to sleep. Nicolas had found the perfect receptacle for her ashes.

PAGE 148: Lisa Fine Textiles Pomona in Red.

PAGES 149–51: Late sixteenth-century gilded-bronze animal-shaped automaton clocks from Augsburg, Germany, wreathed in arrangements of pink and red flowers by Parisian floral designer Eric Chauvin.

PAGE 152: A lion clock with a Nubian attendant.

PAGE 153: A seventeenth-century Florentine pietra dura camel rests on a seventeenth-century French needlepoint.

PAGES 154–55: A collection of seventeenth-century silver from Germany and Italy, sixteenth-century enamels from Limoges and Venice, a seventeenth-century ivory backgammon set, and a fifteenth-century jasper cross from the estate of Yves Saint Laurent, grouped in front of paintings that once adorned the Paris ballroom of Arturo López Willshaw.

PAGES 156–59: Designed by Italian opera director and set designer Pier Luigi Pizzi, the Kugels' library is Pizzi's first private architectural work.

PAGE 160: A seventeenth-century Sicilian embroidery of a garden.

ROSE TARLOW

LOS ANGELES

Rose Tarlow is a giant in the world of interior design. Ironically, she is petite, self-effacing, and rarely talks about herself. I first met her when we were seated next to each other on a plane from London to Venice. During the short flight, we discussed her coveted poodles, Archie and Clarence, bemoaned the inconvenience of modern travel, and wondered why we ever leave our home or our dogs!

Rose's Los Angeles home is a reflection of her personality—authentic, subtle, and elegant. With no one to answer to, she designed and built this jewel box of a house in a mere fourteen months. As in all her projects, nothing is contrived, and the rooms are cozy and comfortable. There are chairs with good light for reading, and side tables and coffee tables within easy reach for setting down a drink. As a designer, an antiques dealer, and a creator of wallpapers, furniture, and fabrics,

Rose is a master at creating the everyday luxury of living.

Good wood and simple furniture are the foundation of her design sensibility. To give the newly constructed house genuine Old World charm, she imported antique salvage materials. Heavy oak beams from an eleventh-century church in England, a pair of eighteenth-century French oak doors, and an entire eighteenth-century French pine room came first, followed by old hardware, seventeenth-century slate, and very old stone for the floors. Rooms bathed in natural light, a mix of old and new textiles and tactile surfaces, the interplay of metal, stone, and wood, and a collection of treasured objects found in her favorite antiques shops and flea markets throughout Europe all work together in harmony. Rose's home is the embodiment of her credo, "A sophisticated room is simple in form and line. Its quality and elegance are subtle."

PAGE 182: Lisa Fine Textiles Lee Stripe in Green.

PAGE 183: Resting on the mantel is a large drawing by Jean Cocteau that he drew on a wall in Paris. That section of the wall was removed and framed.

PAGES 184–85: Balance and comfort with an emphasis on light and texture are signatures of Rose Tarlow's design, as her Los Angles living room attests. The table and floor lamps, uniformly dressed in cream-colored shades, cast soft light in the evening. The furniture is upholstered in fabrics of varying textures and tones of ivory and cream.

PAGE 186: One of Rose's many treasures is this pair of blue-and-white tiles. "They are the oldest I have ever seen and are actually small works of art," she says.

PAGE 187: A collection of antique English pewter chargers, treen plates, and a lingam vessel filled with rare painted-tole leaves is displayed in the dining room.

PAGES 188–89: When entertaining, Tarlow prefers well-worn accessories, different in material and character, and mixes simple, precious, and primitive pieces to create an atmosphere resembling a Dutch still life. White napkins are so large that they reach the old stone floor once draped over her guests' laps, and silver-domed serving dishes with ivory handles never seem pretentious in the rustic dining room. This juxtaposition of the humble with the refined is magically Rose.

PAGE 190: The kitchen was designed around an exceptionally large seventeenth-century French cabinet.

PAGE 191: In the kitchen, a favorite place for dinner parties, a seventeenth-century English oak table is surrounded by a collection of seventeenth-century English and Welsh chairs.

PAGE 192: The master bedroom is a stunning example of Rose's sophisticated play with light, color, and texture: the sunlight streaming in through the floor-to-ceiling windows, the eighteenth-century French boiserie walls, the lacquered bed with the hammered-satin canopy, and the chintz curtains.

LEE RADZIWILL

NEW YORK

The late Lee Radziwell was an artist and an original bohemian. She infused poetry and beauty into everything she touched, which is probably why such luminaries as Rudolf Nureyev and Truman Capote were inspired by her company. I first met Lee through my friend Alejandra Cicognani when we were both living in Paris. Once a week we had lunch or dinner at Le Voltaire or the fashionable bistro Ferdi.

Lee's razor-sharp wit and unerring perceptions and observations were as captivating as her legendary elegance and style. She loved pink peonies, botanical drawings, unique objects. I once admired a small portrait of a deer that she had found in an antiques store on the Left Bank. "I'm constantly falling in love with objects and they follow me around the world," she acknowledged breezily. Yet everything in Lee's world was scrupulously edited—her words, her wardrobe, and her interiors. As the renowned tastemaker Diana Vreeland said, "Elegance is refusal."

The first thing you saw when you walked into Lee's New York apartment was her collection of nineteenth-century Indian paintings on glass. Lee had spotted them when she was newly married and living in London. Without a second thought, she purchased the entire set. Although Lee often bought on impulse and did not deliberately amass items of particular periods or subjects, her apartment reflected the discriminating eye of a collector.

Lee and I shared a passion for animals and an infatuation with the exotic. Lee traveled the world and along the way bought whatever she fell in love with. In her apartment, there was a greyhound from Mallet in London, an eighteenth-century camel from a crèche scene in Rome, two carved-ivory pigs from India. Restrained yet lush, her apartment's décor was an ideal backdrop for objects collected solely by instinct.

Lee's rooms were essentially traditional with touches of "the bizarre, exotic, and delicious." She believed that "taste is an emotion" and rooms should always have "light and life."

Her bookshelves were filled with Wilde, Turgenev, Balzac, Tolstoy, Dumas, Sand, biographies of Peter the Great and Ivan the Terrible . . . Next to the bookshelves, in front of the living room fireplace, a small card table draped in a vintage Yves Saint Laurent scarf from his Russian collection would be set for lunch. The world Lee created felt so removed from New York, even though it was on East 72nd Street.

PAGE 174: Lisa Fine Textiles Rambagh Reverse in Jungle.

PAGE 175: A small painting of a deer that Lee saw in an antiques shop window on the Left Bank in Paris stands behind a pair of carved-ivory pigs from India.

PAGE 176: A rare collection of Indian paintings on glass hangs in the entrance hall.

PAGE 177: A card table is set for lunch with a vintage Yves Saint Laurent scarf serving as a tablecloth. Lee always had touches of pink and red in her linens, porcelain, and glassware.

PAGES 178–79: The living room's ivory linen walls, sofas, and ottoman serve as a soothing backdrop for the many objects and paintings she collected. An eighteenth-century camel from a crèche scene in Rome presides over the room.

PAGE 180: One of the Indian paintings on glass.

PAGE 181: One of a series of Indian portraits that hangs in the dining room.

PAGES 182–83: Lee worked with Renzo Mongiardino on the interiors of many of her homes. His influence is best seen in her dining room, where she cut a striped fabric on the diagonal to create diamond "frames" that enhance her collection of Indian portraits.

PAGES 184–85: Formerly the television room, this storage space contains two of Lee's favorite prints. The chinoiserie fabric on the sofa appeared in every house and apartment that she lived in.

PAGES 186–87: A classic stripe covers the walls and recamier sofa in the sitting room, which is bathed in sunlight most of the day.

PAGE 188: A soft pink, green, and cream canopy stripe covers every wall and piece of furniture in the master bedroom. A mirror by Paris designer Hervé Van der Straeten hangs over the mantel.

FARAWAY PLACES

AT HOME IN PARIS

After my first trip to India, I returned to Paris and a new, empty apartment with bare white walls. The multicolored block prints I'd seen in Jaipur, the golden brocades in Varanasi, and the elaborate mirror embroidery in Kutch had been so overwhelming that I decided to focus my attention first on choosing solid colors for the apartment and leave patterns for later. I knew that I wanted to replicate the pinks and oranges of India. For the living room, I eventually settled on Sanderson's Pink Allure, and for my bedroom I tried to match the mango orange of a court costume in a miniature painting. Then I found yards of pink, orange, and bronze silk taffeta, which the venerable *ensemblier* Decour cut into wide strips and fashioned into striped curtains for the main sitting room. Although layers of patterns followed, shades of pink and orange predominated in both the sitting room and the bedroom.

The tented salon with red velvet banquettes lining the periphery was the room that no one ever wanted to leave. Spontaneous dinners there were one of the great pleasures of my life in Paris. A large, low wooden table in the center served as a dining table, around which everyone sat on footstools covered in antique Moroccan embroidery. A candlelit chandelier from a Moroccan synagogue, found at the Marché aux Puces, Paris's main flea market, often dripped candle wax onto the table far into the wee hours. I had been obsessed with red velvet banquettes since childhood; they reminded me of favorite restaurants and special occasions, including my first martini at Quo Vadis in New York.

Another obsession of mine is tents. On that first trip to India, I went to the camel festival in Jaisalmer, where I stayed in a tented camp. At that time, Jaisalmer had not yet been developed for tourism, and a tented camp was more reliable than a hotel. The fabrics of the tents were all unique, each a cotton block print of a Kashmir paisley or an Indian flower in unexpected and vibrant color combinations. I left knowing that in some form or other, drawing inspiration from the tent camps of Jaisalmer, the tented rooms of Renzo Mongiardino, and the renowned tent of Tipu Sultan, I would tent a room. I took the advice of some frugal but stylish English friends and went to Simrane on rue Jacob, where I found some Indian block-print sheets to tent the salon.

mariette lydis
paris

Photography for this chapter by Ivan Terestchenko and Simon Upton.

PAGE 192: Lisa Fine Textiles Lahore in Apricot.

PAGE 193: The pink, orange, and bronze silk taffeta curtains were made by Decour in Paris by sewing wide stripes of the three colors together. The walls, painted in Sanderson's Pink Allure, and the burnt orange in the Turkish kilim contribute to the India-inspired pink-and-orange palette.

PAGES 194–95: In the main sitting room, a nineteenth-century Dutch chinoiserie screen dominates the wall behind the ten-foot-long aubergine velvet sofa, which is flanked by brown-lacquered end tables with gilded tree-branch legs holding stacks of art and design books. This room is the center of the apartment. Sets of large French doors open onto the master bedroom, the tented salon, and the mirrored dining room/entrance hall.

PAGES 196–97: The painting above the fireplace is a portrait of Malula, my Wheaten Terrier, by New York artist Joe Andoe. It was a gift from Mike Kempner. To the left is a gouache of Scarlet O'Hara, *Having Taking Leave*, by Kara Walker. To the right are two architectural drawings from Charles Plante, a silhouette from Kenneth Neame, and a Company School miniature of a Calcutta house from Martyn Gregory in London.

PAGES 198–99: The salon was tented by Decour with block-print sheets from Simrane on rue Jacob. The chandelier, from a Moroccan synagogue, was found at the Marché aux Puces in Paris. The large, low table is surrounded by stools covered in Moroccan embroidery and suzanis from Uzbekistan. The English Regency snake mirror is a traditional touch yet still in keeping with room's exotic atmosphere.

PAGES 200–201: Marking the corners of the small square mirrors that cover the walls of the entrance/dining room is an assortment of crystal flowers from the Marché aux Puces. A series of verre églomisé Chinese paintings hangs over the mirrored walls. The crystal chandelier's soft candlelight and its reflection in the mirrored walls created a magical atmosphere for dinner parties. The black-lacquered dining table and chairs are from Maison Jansen.

PAGES 202–3: In the master bedroom, the large pink silk panels on the walls were hand dyed in a village outside of Jodhpur and serve as a dramatic backdrop to the Mughal-inspired embroidery on the headboard. The touches of green accent pieces—the lacquered bedside tables, the silk-upholstered chaise, and the frames on the Gio Ponti astrological mirrors—echo the lush green courtyard seen through the large French windows. The shades of pink, coral, and lilac were all inspired by trips to India and colors in Indian miniature painting.

PAGE 204: A lithograph of a cabaret dancer performing with a poodle and two terriers is by Austrian artist Mariette Lydis.

JOHN STEPHANIDIS

PATMOS

I will never forget the first time I was invited to dinner at interior designer John Stefanidis's house in Patmos, one of the islands in the Dodecanese. The evening began with vodka and fresh watermelon juice on a garden terrace shaded by citrus and olive trees. Erudite and charming, John is captivating. I could easily imagine he and his partner, British artist Teddy Millington-Drake, discovering Patmos long before it was fashionable and falling in love with a seventeenth-century house that had no running water or electricity.

Born in Alexandria, Egypt, Stefanidis understands the Mediterranean. Its light, colors, and nature are the prevailing inspirations. All the walls of the house, inside and out, are whitewashed to reflect light and deflect heat. The colors are the blues of the sea and sky, and the interior blends seamlessly into the exterior. Rooms open to terraces, terraces flow into gardens, gardens expand into farmland. The fragrance of jasmine, roses, and gardenias fills the air.

Stefanidis mixes local wood furniture with his collection of Anglo-Indian, Venetian, and English pieces. Layers of Greek and Ottoman embroidery pillows are paired with Indian textiles and Turkish rugs. Teddy Millington-Drake's watercolors of ancient temples and monuments hang amid framed pages from a book of Indian costumes. Stefanidis's house is much like his personality—worldly yet effortlessly relaxed and engaging. As he wrote in his book *An Island Sanctuary*, "A house, your living space, is a sanctuary. Your bed is where you dream. Your kitchen is where you drink coffee or juice, eat breakfast, perhaps lunch or dinner too. Whether it is a room, a house, an apartment, or a loft in Paris, New York, Rio or Mumbai, your sanctuary reflects your personality."

PAGE 206: Lisa Fine Textiles Ayesha in Sapphire.

PAGE 207: The Plumbago Terrace, shaded by olive trees and cypresses, is a magical place for afternoon tea or evening cocktails. It looks out on an herb garden terrace with beds of mint, thyme, parsley, coriander, and arugula. Pots of white *agapanthus* and trailing *pelargonium* add to the lush Mediterranean atmosphere.

PAGE 208: This sitting room features two John Stefanidis Rothschild chairs, loosely slipcovered in a crisp blue-and-white cotton stripe, an eighteenth-century gilt Venetian mirror, and an Indian chest inlaid with ivory.

PAGE 209: The small blue table with red trim is a Stefanidis design. Others in various colors are seen throughout the house.

PAGES 210–11: The double doors with glazed panels are an architectural feature of many houses on the island. The Mughal chest was sent from India to England in the 1820s. The chair is eighteenth-century Italian Baroque.

PAGES 212–13: In this sitting alcove, almost everything on the walls is either Indian or inspired by India: Teddy Millington-Drake's watercolors of south Indian temples, miniatures of Indian gods, costume designs of Indian castes, mirrors framed in gold passementerie. The embroidered pillows on the wall-to-wall sofa are from Patmos, Rhodes, and Anatolia.

PAGE 214: A simple trestle table made on the island serves as a desk.

PAGE 215: Stefanidis found the elaborately carved, eighteenth-century Tuscan mirror in Rome. The block print from Rajasthan covering the banquette beneath the mirror and the natural blue, red, and ochre of the kilim add touches of organic color.

PAGES 216–17: In the main sitting room, everything is white, nutmeg brown, and copper. Cotton mattresses rest on Empire-style sofas. Large double windows with shutters of local wood, typical of the island, open to farmland and the ocean beyond.

PAGE 218: This coffee table was painted by a local fisherman in a naïve style.

PAGE 219: A plate rack displays a collection of Teddy Millington-Drake's ceramic plates in primary colors.

PAGES 220–21: A small sitting room that opens onto the breakfast terrace is furnished with a typical local wood sofa with a white cotton mattress. The window ledge holds a collection of shells from the Greek islands and white stone from Aspronisi, an island in the Santorini archipelago renowned for its white cliffs.

PAGE 222: The nineteenth-century four-poster bed is brass and painted metal. The fifty-year-old bed hangings have hand-crocheted hems.

PAGE 223: Vintage hand-painted plates from Samos rest on the sky-blue shelves in the master bathroom. The trellis-fronted cabinet is reminiscent of the latticework found in the harems of Constantinople, Cairo, and Damascus and popular in the islands of the Dodecanese when it was under Turkish domination.

PAGE 224: Detail of the intricate ivory inlay on the Mughal chest. Images of flora and fauna were popular themes among the Mughals, who were inspired by the lush gardens of Persia.

LUISA BECCARIA

SICILY

Like a fairy-tale castle, Castelluccio rises amid the almond and olive groves just south of the Baroque Sicilian city of Noto on the Ionian Sea. The first time I went to Castelluccio was to celebrate the twenty-fifth wedding anniversary of Luisa Beccaria and her husband, Lucio Bonaccorsi. A series of long, candlelit picnic-like tables covered with white linen tablecloths stretched beneath an allée of olive trees with small candles cascading from their branches. The magical setting harked back to the eighteenth century, when the noble Bonaccorsi family built Castelluccio.

Luisa and her daughters, Lucilla, Lucrezia, and Luna, all statuesque beauties with raven hair and blue eyes, wore off-the-shoulder garden-inspired gowns from Luisa Beccaria's collection. A Milan-based fashion designer, Luisa creates clothes that are always romantic, ethereal, and reminiscent of a bygone era, like Castelluccio. The following day, a lunch of homemade pastas and local delicacies was served buffet-style for the more than three hundred guests, who had been dancing until three in the morning under mirrored disco balls hanging from the almond trees.

Luisa, Lucio, and their five children spend many holidays in this bucolic paradise. In Milan, the three eldest children, Lucilla, Lucrezia, and Ludovico, have opened LùBar, a Sicilian bistro, which brings the rustic, artistic, and relaxed atmosphere, as well as the olives, the olive oil, and the almonds of Castelluccio to the city.

PAGE 226: Lisa Fine Textiles Noor in Jade.

PAGE 227: Purple bougainvillea beautifies the courtyard entrance to the kitchen and pantry.

PAGE 228: Assorted hand-painted ceramic cacti and candlesticks are scattered on an ivory, hand-crocheted tablecloth, all made in Sicily for Luisa Beccaria's tabletop collection.

PAGE 229: Lilacs are everywhere in Beccaria's world, from the lush blooms surrounding Castellluccio to the many hues of the flower in her silk and chiffon dresses.

PAGES 230–31: Closets are filled with romantic, floral-print chiffon, silk, and lace dresses, all reflecting the soft pinks, greens, lilacs, and sky blues found in the gardens outside.

PAGE 232: A collection of Catholic saints in gilt frames hangs from velvet ribbons.

PAGE 233: The entrance to the family chapel, which is adjacent to the house.

PAGES 234–35: The olive grove where the branches are often dotted with candles for evening celebrations and dinners.

PAGE 236: A view of the eighteenth-century Bonaccorsi family seat, Castelluccio.

JAMIE CREEL AND MARCO SCARANI

TANGIER

The first time I went to Dar Zero, I felt like I had entered a setting straight out of the *Arabian Nights*. Crowning its rooftop overlooking Tangier was a Berber tent lined with divans covered in Moroccan rugs and a kaleidoscope of embroidered pillows. Nomadic tribesmen in native costume performed acrobatics with flaming torches, while young Muslim boys danced to the rhythm of crashing cymbals and beating drums. Dar Zero's owner, the legendary Parisian designer Charles Sevigny, and Yves Vidal, the president of Knoll, created a surreal fantasy, blithely mixing 1970s furniture with crafts from villages and markets around Morocco. Today's owners, Jamie Creel and Marco Scarani, have channeled the same sensibility, paying tribute to both North African culture and their European roots. The original Knoll furniture and French 1970s art remain, constantly augmented by their ever-growing collection of artisanal crafts.

With its views of the Strait of Gibraltar, gritty markets against the backdrop of beautiful beaches, Islamic architecture, and daily calls of the muezzins, Tangier has always attracted the artistic and the literary, the iconoclastic and the eccentric. Jamie and Marco fell in love with both the city and Dar Zero. They divide their time between Paris, New York, and Tangier when not traveling in search of treasures for their Upper East Side store, Creel and Gow, a contemporary twist on the Renaissance concept of a cabinet of curiosities.

The idea for Creel and Gow was conceived while they were on a boat in the Galapagos Islands. Although Jamie and Marco collect eighteenth-century and mid-century modern French furniture, their passion is natural history. In their store and in their homes, one finds everything from narwhal tusks, taxidermy peacocks, and ostrich eggs, to a wide assortment of rare minerals and fossils and an array of artisanal decorative objects and ceramics from around the world.

PAGE 238: Lisa Fine Textiles Ayesha in Spinel.

PAGE 239: The entrance gallery at Dar Zero is adorned with nineteenth-century Moroccan candlesticks from mosques, early twentieth-century lanterns, and a collection of rustic Spanish ceramics. The chairs are sixteenth-century French.

PAGES 240–41: The rooftop overlooking the Casbah and the Strait of Gibraltar, the passageway between Africa and Europe since Phoenician times, reflects the Ottoman heritage of the port with classic Moroccan tribal rugs and divans covered in locally woven textiles. Moroccan lanterns of all sizes and shapes with multicolored glass panes are scattered around, in anticipation of being lit at night.

PAGES 242–43: The courtyard of Dar Zero, redesigned by Charles Sevigny, who added many of the traditional Moroccan architectural details.

PAGE 244: A collection of late nineteenth- and early twentieth-century Moroccan hammered-metal boxes, French pewter plates, and English teacups.

PAGE 245: Nineteenth-century Moroccan carved and painted doors came from Barbara Hutton's house in Tangier. The chandelier is French Directoire.

PAGES 246–47: The library, designed by Charles Sevigny, features early nineteenth-century Moroccan painted panels and doors. The eighteenth-century wingback chair is upholstered in a woven fabric from the Fondouk Chejra (Weaver's Market) in Tangier.

PAGES 248: In the breakfast room, a 1950s Saarinen Tulip table is painted bright red. The trellis-back chairs and cabinet, inspired by Moroccan mashrabiya, were designed by Charles Sevigny.

PAGE 249: The original rare Qajar portrait was sold at Christie's in 2008 at the auction of the Charles Sevigny/Yves Vidal Collection. Christie's had this copy made to replace it.

PAGES 250–51: In one of the bedrooms, the curtains are Lisa Fine Textiles Ayesha Panel in Spinel. The orange headboard and bed coverlet were handwoven at the Fondouk Chejra in Tangier. The throw at the end of the bed is Lisa Fine Textiles Ayesha in Spinel.

PAGES 252–53: An entertaining pavilion with wraparound divans and large jali-screened windows was designed by Marco Scarani and built in 2018. The cushions are covered in Lisa Fine Textiles Cambay in Indian Ocean.

PAGE 254: The pillows on the small cream sofa are covered in Carolina Irving Textiles Almaty Velvet and Indian Flower. The borders of the cream curtains are Lisa Fine Textiles Cambay in Indian Ocean.

LULU LYTLE

LONDON

The first time I saw Lulu Lytle's daughter Bunny's twin bed draped in a pink printed cotton with a red Indian chintz quilt, I knew we were kindred spirits. Lulu shares my passion for madder reds and pinks, Qajar portraits, and exotic animals, particularly camels. A textile designer and founder of the home furnishings shop Soane on London's Pimilco Road, Lulu, like me, finds inspiration along the Silk Road.

Lulu first went to Mongolia as a volunteer for the Wild Camel Protection Foundation to help save the beloved and rare two-hump camels indigenous to Mongolia and China. Depictions of camels and other exotic creatures can be found throughout her Bayswater apartment. A large Tibetan tiger, once a rug, now dominates the library wall over a suzani-upholstered sofa. A bronze sculpture of a camel, a naïve watercolor

of a zebra, and a large watercolor of a rhinoceros are among the menagerie of animals scattered throughout the apartment.

A sizable collection of antique textiles and paintings from India, Turkey, Persia, Central Asia, and the Middle East is interspersed among her own designs. An early handwoven ikat of natural dyes from Uzbekistan's Ferghana Valley hangs over her Lotus Palmette wallpaper, inspired by a sixteenth-century Safavid woven silk velvet. A nineteenth-century Qajar portrait of a Persian prince hangs on her Qajar Stripe wall covering, inspired by an antique textile made in Lancashire for the Persian market. Several tables are covered with Indian palampores. A collection of English Sheffield plate, including tagine dishes reminiscent of the domes and minarets of Samarkand, lines the shelves on the turquoise-tiled kitchen walls.

THE TOPKAPI SARAY MUSEUM
Architecture: the Harem and other buildings

te World of Yves Saint Laurent & Pierre Bergé

PAGE 256: Lisa Fine Textiles Bagan in Cinnabar.

PAGE 257: A portrait of Lulu's three children is by Charlotte Johnstone. Panther, the family whippet, lounges on the sofa, upholstered in Soane's Old Flax.

PAGES 258–59: The hand-painted, fern-inspired wallpaper is Osmunda Silhouette from Soane. The naïve watercolor of the zebra was painted by Lulu's daughter Bunny when she was eight years old.

PAGES 260–61: In the living room, the nineteenth-century German watercolor of a rhinoceros comes from the collection of legendary shoe designer Roger Vivier. The Tuileries sofa and the Horus ottoman are by Soane. The carpet is by Veedon Fleece.

PAGE 262: In the dining room, a nineteenth-century Qajar painting of a prince and his attendants hangs on Lulu's Qajar Stripe wall covering. Below is a nineteenth-century calamander shelf holding a collection of old candlesticks.

PAGE 263: In the library, an eighteenth-century painting of an Indian maharaja hunting tigers hangs over the fireplace, which is flanked by a pair of Soane chairs covered in Soane Damascus Stripe. The walls are covered in Soane hand-blocked Lotus Palmette wallpaper. To the left of the fireplace, a handwoven ikat from Uzbekistan hangs over the wallpaper

PAGES 264–65: A narwhal tusk hangs above a repurposed Tibetan rug, depicting a tiger. The sofa is upholstered in a Central Asian suzani print.

PAGES 266–67: In the kitchen, shelves filled with Sheffield plate articles line the bright turquoise-tiled walls above coral-pink cabinets.

PAGE 268: Lulu's daughter's bed is swathed in Soane Ripple Stripe in Raspberry. The quilt is an Indian chintz.

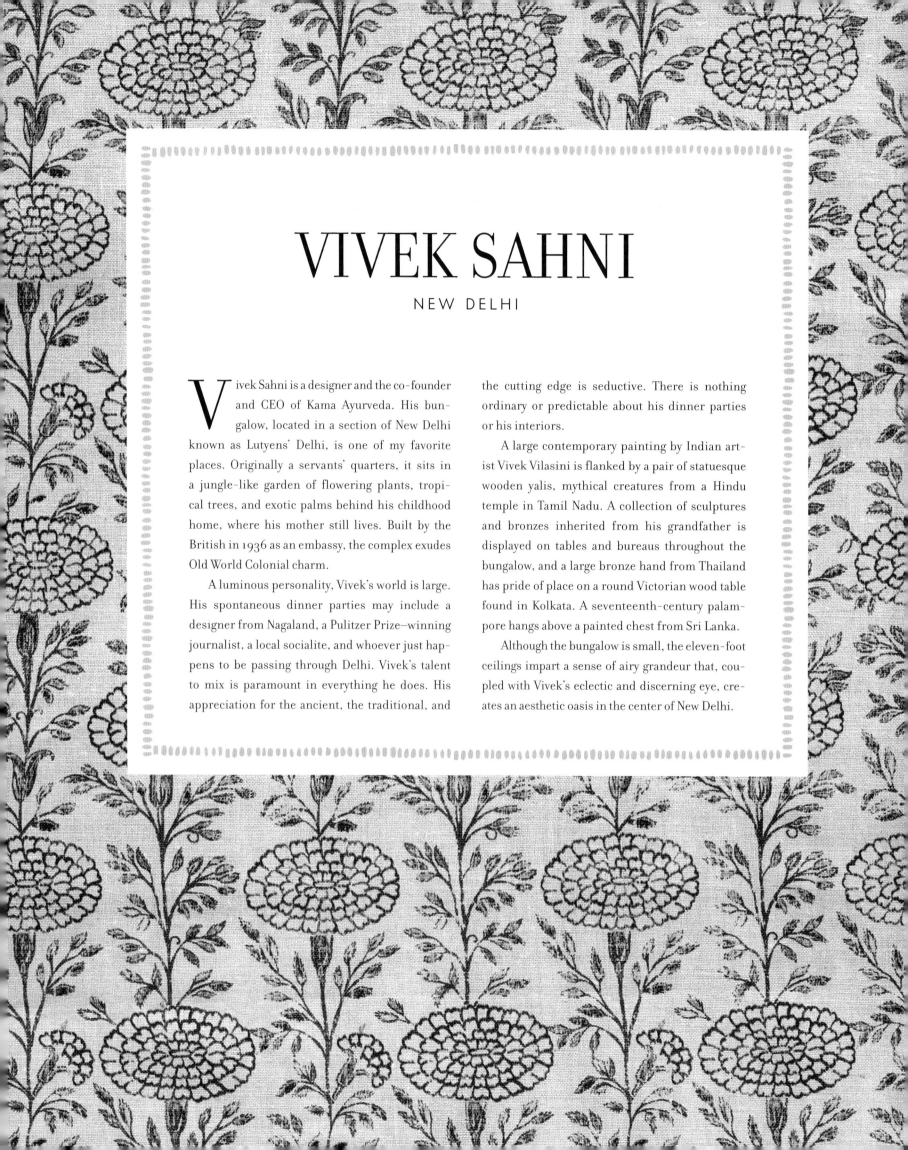

VIVEK SAHNI

NEW DELHI

Vivek Sahni is a designer and the co-founder and CEO of Kama Ayurveda. His bungalow, located in a section of New Delhi known as Lutyens' Delhi, is one of my favorite places. Originally a servants' quarters, it sits in a jungle-like garden of flowering plants, tropical trees, and exotic palms behind his childhood home, where his mother still lives. Built by the British in 1936 as an embassy, the complex exudes Old World Colonial charm.

A luminous personality, Vivek's world is large. His spontaneous dinner parties may include a designer from Nagaland, a Pulitzer Prize–winning journalist, a local socialite, and whoever just happens to be passing through Delhi. Vivek's talent to mix is paramount in everything he does. His appreciation for the ancient, the traditional, and the cutting edge is seductive. There is nothing ordinary or predictable about his dinner parties or his interiors.

A large contemporary painting by Indian artist Vivek Vilasini is flanked by a pair of statuesque wooden yalis, mythical creatures from a Hindu temple in Tamil Nadu. A collection of sculptures and bronzes inherited from his grandfather is displayed on tables and bureaus throughout the bungalow, and a large bronze hand from Thailand has pride of place on a round Victorian wood table found in Kolkata. A seventeenth-century palampore hangs above a painted chest from Sri Lanka.

Although the bungalow is small, the eleven-foot ceilings impart a sense of airy grandeur that, coupled with Vivek's eclectic and discerning eye, creates an aesthetic oasis in the center of New Delhi.

PAGE 270: Lisa Fine Textiles Samode in Poppy.

PAGE 271: A bronze hand from Thailand sits on a Victorian table from Kolkata in front of the marble Art Deco–style fireplace. Sahni designed the mantelpiece during the conversion of the former servants' quarters into his home.

PAGES 272–73: The porte cochere of the bungalow, which is nestled in a lush garden filled with palms and frangipanis in the center of Lutyens' Delhi.

PAGES 274–75: A large painting by Indian artist Vivek Vilasini is flanked by two yalis, mythical creatures from a Hindu temple in Tamil Nadu.

PAGES 276–79: In Sahni's dining room, a seventeenth-century palampore hangs over a painted chest from Sri Lanka. Works from his collection of Indian and South Asian sculptures are displayed on every surface: the dining room table, pedestals, consoles, and the chest.

PAGES 280–81: The dining room opens onto the large garden, which gives guests the sensation of being in a tropical jungle in southern Asia, not in the center of New Delhi.

PAGE 282: In the television room, a nineteenth-century Thai Buddha appears to hover among rose water sprinklers and red frangipani flowers from the garden. Vivek's grandfather brought the frangipani trees to India from Bali in the 1950s.

CAROLINA IRVING

PORTUGAL

I first met textile designer Carolina Estrada, soon to become Irving, with landscape designer Madison Cox and artist Konstantin Kakanias almost thirty years ago, when I was working for *Mirabella* magazine. Even then it was clear that all three of them would have meteoric success. A Venezuelan beauty, Carolina grew up in Paris and studied art history and archaeology at L'École du Louvre before moving to New York to work for Sotheby's.

For as long as I have known Carolina, her life has been an endless series of adventures, discoveries, and creative accomplishments. Every year she hikes with the International Dendrology Society across the mountains and fields of such places as Kyrgyzstan, Kazakhstan, and Crete studying rare trees and flowers. Always intrepid and curious, Carolina once took a taxi on her own from Beirut to Damascus, stopping along the way to visit Roman ruins and cafés. No matter where she travels, Carolina finds and embraces the local artisanal crafts. In fact, her passion for the embroidery and ceramics of the Middle East and the Mediterranean has inspired her new business venture, Carolina Irving and Daughters, a collaboration with her two daughters, Olympia and Ariadne.

Six years ago, Carolina found a plot of land in the Alentejo region of Portugal that overlooks rice fields, dunes, and the Atlantic Ocean. An area best known for its umbrella pines and cork oaks, Carolina fell in love with its rustic beauty and simplicity. She built a whitewashed cottage in the style of the native fishermen's dwellings, planted a garden of succulents and pomegranate, lemon, orange, and jacaranda trees, and began her search for the best artisans in Spain and Portugal.

Although Carolina's homes in both Paris and New York have set stylistic standards and been an inspiration for designers around the world, it is in her Portuguese cottage that her originality and creativity are most apparent. Everything is handmade, and much of it she designed herself. Banquettes and chairs display hand-loomed ikats from Mallorca. Beds and tables are covered with hand-embroidered fabrics from a nearby village. Hand-glazed emerald-green tiles native to Portugal cover the floor. Naturally, ceramic plates and candelabras from Carolina Irving and Daughters adorn tables and walls throughout the interior and on the large outdoor terraces that look out over her garden and the rice fields.

PAGE 294: Lisa Fine Textiles Mughal Garden in Ivory.

PAGE 295: The hand-embroidered suzani from Uzbekistan hanging on the wall was a gift from Carolina's friend Christian Louboutin. The console is draped in a handwoven Portuguese fabric, and the emerald-green tiles covering the floor were also handmade in Portugal.

PAGES 296–97: Irving's garden of agaves, cacti, and palms surrounds the cottage, which resembles local fishermen's houses in style.

PAGE 298: A ceramic bull stands on a shelf below a collection of antique blue-and-cream plates from Granada. A linen pillow with a pomegranate print from Carolina Irving Textiles rests on the banquette.

PAGE 299: A collection of vintage terra-cotta plates from Mexico hangs over the fireplace. The tiered table on the left was made in Tangier by Stephan Janson.

PAGES 300–301: A large, hand-embroidered cloth from Crete hangs over the banquette. The pillows are covered in Patmos, a linen stripe from Carolina Irving Textiles.

PAGES 302–3: The open shelves in the kitchen display a collection of terra-cotta plates and bowls by Carolina Irving and Daughters.

PAGES 304–5: The table on one of the terraces is covered with a tablecloth hand-printed in India for Carolina Irving and Daughters, and the candlesticks were handmade in Portugal for Carolina Irving and Daughters.

PAGES 306–7: It is almost sunset on the terrace facing the open rice fields.

PAGE 308: The table on the terrace overlooking the rice fields is set with Portuguese handwoven placemats, napkins, and terra-cotta plates, all from Carolina Irving and Daughters.

SOURCES

ANTIQUES

ALEXANDER DI CARCACI
carcaci.com

LA GALERIE FLORE
galerieflore.com

GALERIE J. KUGEL
galeriekugel.com

JOHN ROSSELLI &
ASSOCIATES
johnrosselliantiques.com

NICK BROCK ANTIQUES
nickbrockantiques.com

R. LOUIS BOFFERDING
DECORATIVE FINE ART
bofferdingnewyork.com

SUNBURY ANTIQUES
sunburyantiques.com

CERAMICS AND
PORCELAIN

CAROLINA IRVING
AND DAUGHTERS
cabanamagazine.com/collections/
carolina-irving-and-daughters

LABORATORIO PARAVICINI
paravicini.it

RICHARD GINORI
richardginori1735.com

GLASSWARE

GIBERTO ARRIVABENE
giberto.it

LAGUNAB
lagunab.com

MOLERIA LOCCHI
locchi.com/en/

HOME ACCESSORIES
AND FURNITURE

AGAIN & AGAIN
againandagain.com

CHARLOTTE MOSS
charlottemoss.com

CREEL AND GOW
creelandgow.com

HOLLYWOOD AT HOME
hollywoodathome.com

JAMES
jamesshowroom.com

JOHN STEFANIDIS
johnstefanidis.com

KRB
krbnyc.com

NICHOLAS HASLAM
nicholashaslam.com

PENNY MORRISON
pennymorrison.com

ROSE TARLOW
MELROSE HOUSE
rosetarlow.com

SAMURAI EXPORTS
samuraiexports.com

SOANE
soane.co.uk

PAINTINGS AND PRINTS

CHARLES PLANTE FINE ARTS
watercolours-drawings.com/

DANZIGER GALLERY
danzigergallery.com

GALLERY 29
gallery29sundernagar.com

MARTYN GREGORY GALLERY
martyngregory.com

RUGS AND DHURRIES

ABRASH
abrashrugs.com

FLITTERMAN COLLECTION
flittermancollection.com

JAMAL'S RUG COLLECTION
jamrug.com

SAMURAI EXPORTS
samuraiexports.com

TABLETOP

CABANA
cabanagloballuxe.com

GOOD EARTH
goodearth.in

TEXTILES AND EMBROIDERY

ANDRAAB
andraab.com

ASCRAFT
ascraft.com.au

CHHOTELAL BHARANY
Sunder Nagar Market
New Delhi 110003

CLOTH & KIND
clothandkind.com

THE CLOTH SHOP
theclothshop.com

GOOD EARTH
goodearth.com

HALOGEN INTERNATIONAL
Halogen.co.za

HOLLAND & SHERRY
hollandandsherry.com

JOSS GRAHAM
jossgraham.com

KASHMIR LOOM
kashmirloom.com

LESAGE INTERIEURS
lesageinterieurs.com

LISA FINE TEXTILES
lisafinetextiles.com

PABLO TORRE
INTERIORISMO
pablotorre.es

PEAKS & RAFTERS
memoshowroom.com

SAURASHTRA IMPEX
saurashtra-impex.business.site

SIMRANE
simrane.com/en/

TISSU
tissu.co.nz

TISSUS D'HÉLÈNE
tissusdhelene.co.uk

THE TOILEMAN
thetoileman.com

TRAVIS & COMPANY
travisandcompany.com

WELL MADE HOME
wellmadehome.com

World Monuments

HARRIE T. LINDEBERG AND THE AMERICAN COUNTRY HOUSE

MANSIONS OF CHETTINAD

BHARATH RAMAMRUTHAM | GEORGE MICHELL

A PLACE TO CALL HOME   Gil Schafer III

EXOTIC
ORIENTAL

rover
Bow Wow Edition by Andrew Grant

BERNARD BOUTET DE MON
AT THE ORIGINS OF

To my mother and Pasha

ACKNOWLEDGMENTS

First, I want to thank Mark and Nina Magowan and Miguel Flores-Vianna for their confidence in me and for their enthusiastic response to the concept of the book when I proposed it. What started out as a rather daunting project has been the most memorable and inspiring endeavor, thanks to everyone at Vendome. The Magowans, Beatrice Vincenzini, and Francesco Venturi have been a dream to work with. I have loved every meeting with Celia Fuller, the designer, and Jackie Decter, my editor, who had the patience to deal with me and helped me to realize the book I had envisioned.

I am forever grateful to everyone who agreed to be featured in the book. All are friends and acquaintances of extraordinary talent and vision whom I am constantly learning from: Penny Morrison, Sarah Graham, Charlotte Moss, Christopher Moore, Alexis and Nicolas Kugel, Charlotte and Alexander di Carcaci, Rose Tarlow, the late Lee Radziwill, John Stefanidis, Luisa Beccaria, Jamie Creel and Marco Scarani, LuLu Lytle, Vivek Sahni, Carolina Irving, the Bharany family, Piero Castellini, Katie Ridder.

I owe a great deal to Lisa Miller and Raymundo Alcaraz, who worked with me tirelessly to create my first textile collection. They taught me a lot, and we were always able to laugh and have fun in the process. I also want to thank Sarah Fader, who was instrumental in the early stages, and Michelle Ciriello, who has been the most devoted and hardworking manager of Lisa Fine Textiles.

I thank Jody Hagan and Ana Sanchez, who are always there in Dallas to assist in any way to make things happen. I also want to thank Michelle Payne, who has been with me for more than twenty-five years. She organizes every aspect of my life and business at all times and in all places and circumstances. And I owe a debt of gratitude to David Elfassy, my tech consultant extraordinaire.

I am grateful to Brett Wood, who will travel anywhere with a smile to work with Miguel and help him capture the picture, regardless of time zones, long hours . . .

In the early 1980s, when I moved to New York, I was infatuated with the city and the world of design. Early on, there were several friends who opened doors for me, inspired me with their successes, and as a result changed the course of my life. I want to thank Sam Blount, Bill Hamilton, Richard Keith Langham, Ann Hall, Marian McEvoy, Madison Cox, and Annette Tapert.

Finally, I am deeply indebted to all the showrooms that carry my textiles, especially John Rosselli and Jonathan Gargiulo of John Rosselli & Associates, and Peter Dunham of Hollywood at Home, who were the first to offer my very small textile collection in their showrooms.

Lisa Fine

Near & Far: Interiors I Love
First published in 2019 by The Vendome Press
Vendome is a registered trademark of The Vendome Press, LLC

NEW YORK
Suite 2043
244 Fifth Avenue
New York, NY 10001

LONDON
63 Edith Grove
London,
SW10 0LB, UK

www.vendomepress.com

Distributed in North America by Abrams Books
Distributed in the United Kingdom, and the rest of the world,
by Thames & Hudson

ISBN 978-0-86565-365-8

PUBLISHERS:
Beatrice Vincenzini, Mark Magowan, and Francesco Venturi
EDITOR: Jacqueline Decter
PRODUCTION DIRECTOR: Jim Spivey
PREPRESS COLOR MANAGER: Dana Cole
DESIGNER: Celia Fuller

Library of Congress Cataloging-in-Publication Data
available upon request

Printed and bound in China by 1010 Printing International Ltd.
FIRST PRINTING

Photo Credits
All photos by Miguel Flores-Vianna, with the exception of the following:
Håkan Groth: p. 10
Eric Piasecki: p. 13
Ivan Terestchenko: pp. 193, 201, 204
Simon Upton: pp. 194–200, 202–3

ENDPAPERS: Lisa Fine Textiles Mughal Garden in Natural.
PAGE 2: Detail of my New York living room (see also pages 124–25).
PAGES 4–5: Lisa Fine Textiles Cochin in Burnt Sugar.
PAGE 6: A late nineteenth-century hand-embroidered Kashmiri shawl from the Bharany Collection.
PAGES 18–19: Lisa Fine Textiles Nicobar in Cocoa.
PAGES 120–21: Lisa Fine Textiles Lee in Red.

PAGES 190–91: Lisa Fine Textiles Kalindi in Indigo.
PAGE 302: The wide-ranging assortment of pillows on the banquette in my New York living room includes a yellow-dotted silk ikat from Seref Ozen in Istanbul, an "Almaty" velvet ikat from Carolina Irving Textiles, and a cotton block print from Jaipur.
ABOVE: A Company School miniature of a Calcutta house from Martyn Gregory.